BOSTON POEMS

SARAH-JANE BURTON

SARAH-JANE BURTON

BOSTON POEMS

CORDITE BOOKS 06 04

First printed in 2025
by Cordite Publishing Inc.

PO Box 58
Castlemaine 3450
Victoria, Australia
cordite.org.au | corditebooks.org.au

National Library of Australia
Cataloguing-in-Publication:

Burton, Sarah-Jane
Boston Poems
978-0-6457616-7-2 paperback
I. Title.
A821.3

Poetry set in Lora 10 / 15
Cover design by Zoë Sadokierski
Text design by Kent MacCarter and Zoë Sadokierski
Printed and bound by McPhersons in Maryborough, Victoria

 Cordite Publishing Inc. thanks Sarah-Jane Burton, Alex Creece and Heather Clark for their input during the production of this book.

10 9 8 7 6 5 4 3 2 1

For Arielle, my next chapter.

CONTENTS

PREFACE xi

INTRODUCTION xiii

1

On Becoming a Poet 3
America 4
Nullius and Cervisia 6
Copley Square 7
The Kindness of Ravens 8
Amtrak 12
Ether Dome 14
Coffee 15
On the T. Part 1 16
Loving Lowell 18
Freedom Trail North 20
My Father's Feet 21

2

Enter Boston 25

3

In the Company of Poets 39
Diana 40
Professor John Holmes 42
Melancholy Lady 43
Mapping Elizabeth 47
Treasures 48
Lizzie and Cal 50
Arrowroot 52

4

On the T. Part 2 59
Kind of Like Her 60
Sonnet Remembering You 61
Lines 62
The Urban Literate 63
Memory Book 64
Lobotomy 67
Veritas 68
Pages 69

ACKNOWLEDGEMENTS 71

PREFACE

I'd never been to Boston when I started researching the city for my graduate studies. But when looking for connections between the American poets I adored, it always came back to this place and space. This historic city on a hill drew writers toward it like a beacon, and eventually it drew me there too.

The poems in this book were then born from the intersection of cobblestone and my developing consciousness, where the weight of history met the urgency of my present moments. Boston became both my muse and my mirror during the years I spent researching it, walking its streets, riding its trains, and absorbing the stories, dreams, and echoes of history that spilled from coffee shops and park benches, from redbrick homes and expansive college campuses.

What began as fragments scribbled in notebooks in jetlagged hazes grew into an extended love letter to a city that became my second home across a decade of arrivals and departures.

Writing these poems felt like archaeological work. I was uncovering layers of meaning beneath the familiar, but it was a process always complicated by the foreign perspective and family history I brought with me from Australia. This included my Indigenous heritage as well as the grief, depressions and anxieties I was navigating during parts of this time.

This collection spans seasons of presence and absence, of research and passion that brought me back, and then the personal tides that pulled me away. It is not just snapshots of what I saw in Boston, they're also an attempt to capture the person I was becoming while learning to call it home.

INTRODUCTION

In *Boston Poems*, Sarah-Jane Burton conjures the city she came to know intimately while researching the lives and work of Robert Lowell, Sylvia Plath and Anne Sexton. These poems are odes to Boston's grand public spaces, universities, writers and pioneering hospitals. But Boston is also the site of a crushing loneliness. 'Walking in this city of cobblestone / I'm the flaneur, poetess, ingénue / But all I want to do is cry in a foreign bed / And think of you.' The flâneur's confident, Whitmanian sense of optimism continually crashes up against New England's darker, Gothic undercurrents. Burton braids these two psychic elements together in intimate poems whose mournful rhymes speak to eddying silences below the surface. The poems are at once tempered and passionate, painful and exuberant, formal and inventive. With expansive vision, Burton explores Boston, the self, family legacy, intergenerational trauma and poetic confession itself.

These poems are also an homage to the author's native Australia. The backward and forward glances of Burton's Janus-faced vision speaks to belonging and alienation; Boston's history becomes a portal into her own. There are searing elegies to lost parents and lost cultures. 'Memory Book' memorialises her 'father with a poet's soul,' while the tender, Heaney-esque 'Arrowroot' is for her mother:

> *Mumma's little girls*
> you'd say about those flowers
> planting them
> ready
> every spring
> the delicacy of an angel
>
> I'd watch the freckles on the back of your hands
> match the freckles on the back of my hands

Half a world away from Australia, in another colonial city, Burton finds dark parallels between her own indigenous heritage and Native American history. In 'Nullius and Cervesia,' she reflects on this connection and the inheritance that makes alcohol 'poison'. In Massachusetts, a state named after a native tribe, her lineage presents itself in new but familiar contexts: 'Shawmut will you show?'

The city's literary legacies are less fraught. Poems to and about Boston poets like John Holmes, Robert Lowell, Sylvia Plath and Anne Sexton draw from Burton's scholarship. She has a flair for literary echoes, and playfully addresses several American poets in their vernacular. Even as she delights in Plath's and Sexton's rhythms, she questions Lowell's use of his marriage in his poetry. In 'For Lizzie and Cal', she writes:

> There's a line where she holds her pillow to her hollows like a child
> And you do nothing to soothe her ache
> The magnolias bloom and then die in their white
> and you write

Lowell's betrayal of Hardwick in *The Dolphin* suggests the more troubling aspects of American culture itself – greed, grift, and selfishness disguised as individualism. In the collection's final poem, the speaker undercuts her own starry vision as she comes to terms with America. With freedoms curtailed and universities under siege in 2025, American democracy seems on the brink of collapse. 'Boston: buyer beware.' Yet, Burton senses the American spirit still stirring in the libraries and archives of her adopted city, where 'woodgrain glows under pages.' She may find herself, again, 'in the sitting room reading poetry.'

—Heather Clark

1

On Becoming a Poet

Worcester, Harvard, Trowbridge and fanfare
It's $12.99
Half off, summertime
Will I find my voice in this?
Time locating rhyme.

Redbrick and shingle
Blue ovals saying others were here
For me, it's topsy-turvy
Upside down
Beneath shingled sounds.

Shaking. My nights are days and mornings
Nights
Mourning, I spin outward and within
Jetlagged beyond reason, I pop the gummies, and I begin.

The fall
The crush
O what might is night. It blends out of day.

I wake finally

Walking in this city of cobblestone
I'm the flâneur, poetess, ingénue.

But all I want to do is cry in a foreign bed
And think of you.

America

Backpacks.
Fanny packs.
Flip-flops.
Birkenstock.

This place is a wharf of minds.
On those rafts of thinking
I'm left

behind. Tanned skins kissed by a different sun.
Bermuda shorts and tank tops blur to one

kaleidoscope and I know
I'm the Old
kind of Navy.

Pummelled by the heat of another hemisphere
I search for Kleenex, tissue thin the light,
and wonder what I am doing, here

under the undulating cobblestones, where
dozens and dozens of echoes moan.
And everyone seems to forget
the palimpsest.

Written on.
Over, over.
Scrawls.

And I crawl
babylike on the sidewalks
under elms.

This unfamiliar ship, my Mayflower
just me, novice at the helm
in waves of solid red brick.
I taste the green.

I jaywalk to fit in and wonder
why the crosswalk figure is always white.

Humming to the sirens, I feel my wires at night.
Within me and outside, I see the grime of
so much pastime.

Nullius and Cervisia

Lagers and longnecks.
Sheds full of hops and taps.
Father always made his own,
brother with canned red and green
ready for the war.

Now on a Boston greenway
I seem to be as far away as physics allows.
From that bottled fear and knowledge,
distilled and instilled, I ask for more.

I've claimed this new place as my own
yet still the loud, dull, beat of a heart in the chest,
sped then slow, knows me best.
Entering the barren childhood lands of before.

I'll always understand the friendship with liquor,
comrade in soothing memory's weather.
The drink and I have been through a lot together
before I closed that dark and heavy beaten door.

We usually keep our distance, we must.
But in this Boston craft brew tiki hut
I press my fingers to glass and wait for the cut.
Like home if I drink three or four more.

Brown paper bag. Bad.
The buzz descends as my cup empties slow.
My genes make this poison.
Shawmut will you show?

Copley Square

Under Trinitarian spires,
I worship John Singleton Copley.
Behind the bends and fens of Back Bay and Boylston
lay the remnants of Art Square.

I trace the past on atlases and gazettes, and it hurts.
I kneel on bricks of the Old South Church,
persecuted behind the Public Library and bright hotel light.
Here lay the ruins of forgotten Boston.

Much missing on the map now, the tourist finds you and your
basics on duck tours as the trolleys trill about.

But the bells ring out in Copley, from the churches
in a city that God hasn't forsaken.
How the missing pieces can't be mistaken,
what time and years and death has taken.

Quatrefoil magic above the eye still glistens,
but it is a rare visitor who takes a moment and listens.
Worshipping John Singleton Copley,
I mull around creative missions.

Painting portraits of those who mattered then,
he abandoned the city for foreign shores.
But he's frozen in the square, in patina now,
more important than before.

The Kindness of Ravens

One morning feeling weary, spectral stanzas spin so eerie
I walk sepulchral spaces on Boston's broken floor.
    While my energy is sapping, a crispy wind starts its rapping
    'It's the Winter coming,' but I'm lacking – lacking a coat at season's door.
Lonely here I wander, old days I sadly ponder, knocking at the season's door.
        But it's only that, and nothing more.

Moments lost to remember, before this bleak November;
And each separate family member leaves their ghost upon the floor.
    I used to wish for bright tomorrows – then deny, I dodged the sorrow
    But my mind would bring things harrowed – sorrow for before –
For the places and the loves, whom I lost before –
        Nameless here forevermore.

And the sullen, saddened burden left in wake of Christly sermons
Killed me – filled me with fine terrors I'd never felt before.
　So to calm my heart its beating, I tried swiftly a retreating,
　'This vision is just dreaming, soon I'll find the door –
It's just my mind that is tricking, tricking that there isn't more –
　　That is it, and nothing more.'

I'd wished I were a little stronger, wished they'd stay a little longer,
'Mother don't leave,' said I, 'and Father, I'll need you forevermore.'
　But life, it passes briefly, and they balanced days so steely,
　And so faintly death it trapped them, then came tapping at my door,
There will always be an ending, you must open wide that door –
　　See the darkness there, and nothing more.

The sky it started leering, long I stood there startled, fearing,
Hurting, aching from the nightmares I'd never dreamt before.
　But my heart it was so broken, and the silence left me frozen,
　There were no words to be spoken just a breathless voice of gore.
'Don't go,' I whispered, and an echo murmured back, no more.
　　Merely this, and nothing more.

I found Boston slowly luring, still the core within me burning,
I'd hear that eerie tapping – tapping louder than before.
  Boarding planes and thinking, new memories slowly linking –
  Let me see then what is out there, this city to explore –
My heart still beats this moment, so this world I can explore –
    Hoping every moment, I'll find a little more.

Landing here amongst white shutters, I'd greet eyes with a stutter,
Then a bird I saw there, flutter, darkened corvid of deathly lore.
  But my soul he did not frighten; for his message would enlighten –
  Daily I'd invite him, welcome perched above my door –
Feathers stretched above me nightly, nightly at my door –
    He would sit, and nothing more.

Persecuted years a hundred, Raven now I find you huddled,
Rebuilding nests that you smuggled – smuggled behind the settler's door.
  Shall I be the same and settle, our raspy voices meddling,
  Two broken souls now betting – betting Boston is our shore.
New England newness proffers, offering us more.
    Quoth the Raven, 'Open doors.'

The Raven never falters, stays there sitting, always watching,
On the crest of Harvard gated, it can open up its door.
And his feathers always hoping, their ebony is smoking,
And the daylight that is beaming throws his shadow on the floor.
I know the Raven knows life's secrets – he has seen behind the door.
He knows my heart is sore.

Across new paths I'm pressing, there are no words expressing,
New beginnings I am seeking, wanting freshness in my core.
Moving forward without knowing, the Raven guides my guessing,
Our wings are clipped from all the falling, silky and so torn.
But bruises keep us going, with our knowledge we see more.
I close a little more.

Later sitting in a library, watching students gesture wildly,
Their bodies moving lithely, unaware of darkened doors.
I try to be forgetful, tell myself, 'Don't be resentful,'
But my pillow tears are dreadful, behind my now-closed door.
No one knows I am still mending, and I'll never stop the thinking,
Is this it – is this all?
I'll always want for something more.

Amtrak

The glow
of Dunkin' D
lures me into
South Station.

Promises of
pumpkin spice,
decadence,
The Summer,
but Fall calls.

Nylon swimsuit, then synthetic sweater weather.
Is nothing pure at all?

Artificial, industrial, commuter central hall.
It promises me Yankee dreams.
New England classic as the trains move
toward lakes, Maine, fishermen on a shore.

These are the places of lobstermen,
skins as hard as shells that reach with mollusc paws.
I dream of green I can only see at dawn,
and ride the train out of Boston once more.

It flickers, this outside perspective.
I'm here but I'm not at all.
Pictures glide past like perfect postcards.
White houses, picket fences,
I'm in suburban awe.

Take me away. Take me away.
Music fills my ears and I'm calm, no defenses.
It's pristine on this Labor Day weekend.
Only dreams on this train line, these shores.

Carparks with grass creeping through.
Is something here pure after all? Crustacean

heat on asphalt
at the new station.
Promised New Hampshire, more
walls and tracked railway floor.
Not a dream
after all.

Ether Dome

'When in distress every man becomes our neighbor'
– Massachusetts General Hospital founding credo, 1810

The hospital
is hardly general
from where I'm perched in Massachusetts.
Bulfinch broad, the coarse granite grains
and fenestration lines align.
Voluted columns wend to tenements
under a fan-lit sky. Towering
scrolls around sterile linoleum for miles.
Fourth floor arrival and there's light everywhere.
Hiding scars and barbs in this circular chair. Decked womb.
I learnt that these spaces were far away,
so no one heard patients scream.
Then a cold October day, 1846
medicine would never again be without a fix.
Come Greek deity, come Akasha, fifth element arise.
From a sponge in a glass-blown bubble,
eternal substance of the night.
The struggle, the trouble, instantly gone.
A crater dropped in the room.
Diethyl ether anaesthesia. Carbon atom oxygen.
A globus sliced in sleep.
What will be next?
Men on moons?
In this room now it all acts so small.
An insignificant place. Nothingness, nothing at all.
No more shrieks from the operating theatre.
The sky lights the room now in a different way.
There's sun inside the cold light of today.

Coffee

Once you were ebony, lucidity in each pour
Refilled hourly you sing for me
Clutching curved white mug
Bringing ideas closer in my eye
Patchwork and spider webs interlocked
Creamer and pie

I drink too much in the hotel lobby
My car is coming at four
I tremble, how do I leave this place of coffee
To drink espresso once more, laughing
I'm shaking from one last pour. At home
I'll be flat and over and white

You still have a spell to hold me
Warm and flowing don't leave
Me yet, but you must, jet
Black
Is your color.

It's my colour.

On the T. Part 1

True masTerpiece in meTal

golden edge

no edging over

grime in the

inlaid arched

enclave of

insurgenT bolTs cold and

so creased new echoes of

bleeps and Taps

sunken arTeries Thump

Through the cold weeps

sleep noT

sweeT as an apple rhubarb pie rapid TransiT line

TasTing like meTal and To The Touch

The cluTch of a seaT

a boy carries his pumpkin

iT's halloween

now

we ride as fall becomes winTer

on The orange line

in This paradise of forgoTTen

Time The welds wail

back and forTh a dance with force

love dark inTo The Tunnels

an ark of arT

Loving Lowell *for Robert Lowell and family*

Box one and two, twenty-three wait for me
fresh with dust, a family tree line and lure.
I owe a ballad, a sonnet, an elegy,
an ode to familial tapestry.

Here, Sevenels looks like built history,
Augustus the fifth of the crimson pure.
Five children should still mean a legacy
to count his cotton coins so carefully.

I pray to Percival the heavenly,
his canals on Mars dropped to the floor.
Fame the star he'd not get the chance to see
from his Arizona observatory.

Now Abbott Lawrence is looking at me,
still growing money behind college doors.
He was seventy-six in thirty-three
dropping the crown of his presidency.

Driving down the road there's still more to see.
Outside Boston, I find them still and sure.
Francis got a town with his silks and tea,
his merchant wealth well spinning violently.

Here's Jack the Gardner, still a Peabody;
Isabella stuffing pearls in a drawer,
always buying art, but she's temporary,
building themselves into apoplexy.

James Russell would be known for poetry.
By the fireside, his writing became lore,
his New England Romantic fantasy
in pages on shelves lasting peacefully.

Aunt Amy looks from Brookline silently
laughing in pearls at fools who stand in awe.
She's robust and smiles so pleasantly,
fine clothes hiding all her tendencies.

I came looking for Robert, finally.
Walking along the Maine seashore,
he reigns over Puritan fallacies.
How I adore his hierarchic privacies.

Here's to dear old Boston, home of beans and cod
and the Lowells, many more.

Freedom Trail North

Best outside Italy
the strings on the box preserve
a treat hardly deserved.
North End cannoli for all.
Modern Mike's taste against the trail.
Real freedom couldn't have foreseen
the stomping sandals with arch support.
I hear the Southern accents and watch people
line and lick the interstate and transcontinental lips.
They saw it on YouTube, it's this and the lobster roll.
Paul Revere's House and the graveyards
keep watch on these new souls.
Folded pamphlets, they waddle
after duck boats
and tour guides, on lines.
Don't venture east or west.
Who knows what they'd find.
A secret door, a grave that wasn't so famous.
Who would want a selfie with that after all.
I crunch on my own cannoli,
from another
better
store.
Stare at thongs that I now call flip-flops
and wonder,
am I just a tourist after all?
I rubbish my thoughts of bins in the trash can.
Drink a soda, no fizzy here.
Then I realise my shoes have arch support.
And Revere sees through me here.

My Father's Feet

Each step I step
I never walk alone
Looking down I see
Beneath the skin, the bone
The shape and memory
Feet side by almost side
His laughter belly deep
Big hearts we could not hide
I have my father's feet
Some say I have his eyes
When the world downs me
I see him by my side
I know that I don't walk alone
With his heart beating huge
I have my father's soul
And sometimes, his pride
The world it shakes me
It takes me down, I know
But I reach back up again
Because I know I can
As I have my father's feet
Each step I take is him
Life demands its toll, and
I look to him to hold
But there's an empty chair
It's cruel Daddy isn't there
But I have my father's feet
When things aren't fair
Sometimes simple words
Such silly little rhymes
Rock me in a nursery
In this great expanse of time
But I know he'd tell me
He's so proud he was mine
I have my father's feet, I know
He wants me to leap
I take each step alone
Like Frost, promises to keep
I have my father's feet

And with them
He'll walk me home

2

Enter Boston

It was the North American summer of 2019, and I was at the Houghton Library, Harvard University. I lifted the lid on a large brown box and was struck down by what the archivist had mentioned the day before. She'd warned me about a certain odour when we'd discussed the advice of the University's environmental team on how to approach the situation at hand. I'd agreed to take, what she'd explained, were significant risks to my own health in order to proceed with my work. My vision quickly caught up with my olfactory system and I saw fine curlicues of mildew decorating the edge of one worn page, poking out of a once-beige manila folder marked 'Correspondence'. Speckles of mould-dust illustrated another sheaf of ragged pages. A bound folder looked as if it had withered beneath the weight of the grey and green powder that covered it. History was intertwining with biology. Paper had met nature. I was researching in archives, experiencing the past through physical material. Searching for stories in histories, in boxes. Looking for voices.

My relationship with Harvard began during my doctoral studies, a little less than 10 years before that summer, when I'd applied for a dissertation grant at the Arthur and Elizabeth Schlesinger Library on the History of Women in America. It was a small financial grant, which dropped significantly after the international taxes. But that, months of savings, along with the help of my home university in Australia, meant that I was able to go. A girl with a dad who could barely read and write – the first in her family to even go to university – was going to Harvard. I was to begin the first stages of my work with archival material. I didn't know what archives really were then, or that over my career such material history would be something I would become so passionate about.

Despite pressure over my academic career to change trajectories due to my Indigenous heritage, my research has very little to do with Indigenous *content*. I don't fight for Indigenous health outcomes, land rights or social equality in my work. I care about these issues, but I don't research them. My skin is pale and my eyes are blue; I don't battle physically to fit into the world because of my family history. But belonging is about more than the physical, and it is rarely certain. In my work, I write about white, privileged, mostly heterosexual, cisgender American poets. I am not pale on the inside. I am passionate about these poets, and this work. Even though he had no idea what written poetry was, my dad had a poet's soul and he gave it to me – he encouraged me to listen to, find and tell stories. Poetry is an oral tradition. It was and is one of the emotional, creative and intellectual places I feel a true sense of home. Improving educational access for all people drives me – not only increasing access to poetry but to educational institutions in general, especially those with purported prestige. I care about people who are learning while struggling to belong. I care about and was taught about the need to spend time connected, about community, respect, humility. I understand the psychological inheritances of trauma, alcoholism and children without parents. I carry all this with me when I turn to the pages in an archive and the poems in a book. I carry this story into the Australian institutions where I work.

I took all of this to Harvard.

Harvard University was named in honour of a gift of books, when its first benefactor, the young minister John Harvard, left his personal library and half his estate to the institution in 1638. Two years after Harvard was founded, it opened the Indian College. One of the current freshman dormitories of Harvard Yard, Matthews Hall, stands where this subset of the university operated from the 1650s into the end of the century. Only five Native American students attended the Indian College at Harvard, but the building was the first brick building of this iconic red brick place. Within its walls was the college's printing press, and it was here that the first Bible in North America was created, an Algonquian translation.

But this time was an early phase of the complicated relationship between the college and Indigenous peoples – a relationship that continues to this day. Controversies are ongoing, including those over collections in Harvard's Peabody Museum of Archaeology and Ethnology, but Harvard is now working towards a different future.

The Peabody Museum is one of the sites on the Harvard campus that is full of archival wonders. It houses anthropological materials from across the globe, including more than 1.2 million individual cultural items, even hundreds of artefacts drawn from Australia and Indigenous peoples on my home continent. I was in awe of the mythology of the place, the cultural and intellectual power, the knowledge.

When I went to Harvard for the first time, I assumed that the gates and doors would open to me as soon as I arrived. But things are never quite this simple. The red brick and undulating cobblestones offered a different landscape, a different kind of country. Complicated connections.

By the time I was working in the Houghton Library with the mouldy boxes in 2019, I'd returned to Harvard many times after that first fellowship. By 2019, it had become familiar. Compared to the Indian

College and the first parts of Harvard, I'd learned that Houghton Library was reasonably young. It was the first custom-built building at a university in the United States specifically designed to house rare books, manuscripts and other archival material. The Harvard Library system and the Peabody are different, but they share an ecosystem. They house the wonders of the archives.

Houghton came into being in 1942 after a former graduate of the university and an active arts patron, Arthur A Houghton Jr, bequeathed the funds required for the unique structure. It followed on from the infamous Harvard Treasure Room, which had been housed in the nearby Widener Library for several decades. The Treasure Room contained various rarities that had been given to the university over several centuries, including medieval manuscripts, early printed books, American maps and rare newspapers from the 18th and 19th centuries. According to an article in *The Harvard Crimson* about the expansion of the Treasure Room in 1929 – when the university was not yet co-educational – the room was described as 'separated from the remainder [of the library] by locked doors.'

'Glass casings have been built over the shelves surrounding the open space, and several tables and chairs [...] placed about the room. These are to be used by men making studies for which facts can be found only in the volumes of the Treasure Room.'

I'd wondered: if women hadn't even entered that space, had Indigenous people?

The Harvard Library system now has a mind-boggling 16.8 million volume university-wide physical collection of books and paper-based archival materials. Many of these are locked and preserved in the HD – the Harvard Depository – another intellectually sacred space, a modern marvel of materials preservation and storage located in Southborough, Massachusetts. The HD is 45 minutes' drive from the main campus and is a huge warehouse that houses roughly half of Harvard's library collections.

Climate-controlled, the HD is a chilly wonderland with 30-foot shelves (a touch over nine metres) and the staff there require forklifts to retrieve many of the items when they are called in to one of Harvard's some seventy library locations for use. The HD has around 50 aisles, each holding 2000 shelves and, on each shelf, hundreds of books. Cultural historian Jeffrey Schnapp poetically explains, amongst those shelves there is a certain type of mystery and magic. He describes how 'a deafening silence reigns in the midst of a universal spectacle of immobility. Books rub up against other books, typefaces touch in secret, imperceptible conversations are carried on, across the shelves and across the centuries that deride the petty illusions of the living.'

My trip in 2019 was my second official and funded fellowship to Harvard across a decade, and this time everything was different. Over the years I have spent at the College working in the collections, I've found my way, found my place and learnt that prestige and privilege comes with struggle and cost, along with many gifts. I finally feel I belong there, in part because of wonderfully supportive communities, including many of those at Houghton. But along the journey to this sense of belonging, I had to wrestle with and learn what an archive was. What my family legacies were, through the illnesses and deaths of both of my parents.

What history was and is. What it means to me.

While a contested academic term, an archive – as I understand it now – is an accumulation of historical records, but it's also more. It is voices and visions, what is said and left unsaid. Often the spaces between physical materials, or the lack of physical materials at all, tells much more.

We need to listen to the silence.

Etymologically, the word archive comes from the Greek *arkhē*, which means a 'beginning', an 'origin', a 'first place'. The shape of this word always echoes in my mind when I first look into boxes and wonder what I'll find. It haunts me when I think of my own family's history – the lack of any paper or 'evidence' of them, the fact that there was a first place that was lost to them and ultimately to me. What do we do when there is no paper in which to find the past?

But like so many stories and oral traditions can be lost to time, so can paper. The mouldy materials I was working with in 2019 had been damaged as the result of a flood in the residential basement that was their former home. Water had made its way into the items and been disguised under the sheaths of paper and cardboard. I'd helped deposit the archives into the Harvard collection around five years earlier, and in those years – even with the HD's impeccable temperature control at a cool 10 degrees Celsius with 35% per cent humidity – once-invisible little seeds of mould, or 'spores', had ferociously taken hold of many of the papers and ephemera so precious to the preservation of this slice of literary history.

The paper had a fragile chemical makeup; the spores had caused destruction and a large part of this particular archive crumbled into dust. As books and paper contain a type of organic matter called cellulose, they are easily eaten by environmental and biological contaminants. These invaders multiply, and knowledge is lost. This metaphor is not lost on me as I take my own story into my work with paper.

The Houghton reading room, like many others across America, is locked and protected with an on-site security guard, ID checks and strict rules. It is always supervised by librarians and archivists. Clearance is required before scholars can enter the room or request materials. All materials are handled with a strict set of protocols including book cradles, special weights to hold the pages, and cotton gloves where necessary. But because my papers had been damaged, I couldn't work in the reading room. Those little seeds would pass like a virus into other materials. I had instead been invited to descend a spiral staircase and had found luxurious-looking wooden doors with brightly polished brass handles leading to the many rooms within Houghton's lower levels. Some of the libraries in the Harvard system are connected by tunnels and corridors under the grounds of Harvard Yard. A secret hideaway. The underground nature of it all makes me think about what is even deeper. The country. The past.

I worked in a room where glass-covered shelves lined the walls and heavy, locked wooden cabinets sat below. I soon learned the sealed shelves and cupboards held Houghton's precious printing and rare graphic arts collection, with most of the heavily adorned books surrounding me dating between 1500 and 1800 AD. I thought about how Indigenous people had lived on the grounds where Harvard stood for many years before that, the Shawmut Peninsula. The tribal homelands of the Massachusett people. There was a continuing presence of the Massachusett, and neighbouring Wampanoag and Nipmuc peoples here, but this grandeur was what stood now. In those spaces, I tried not to forget them – I still try.

To be officially organised and part of an archival environment like Houghton, things need to be 'accessioned' – archivist speak for the process of unpacking, examining, describing and indexing materials. In the *Journal of Archival Organization*, Rachel Searcy describes how the process of accessioning is often one of the 'least visible', least 'discussed', and rarely 'critically examined activities' of the professional archivist, but this hidden practice is crucial to ensuring these items are properly stored and used. Usually, fully accessioned collections will have a library catalogue entry and a finding aid that details information about what is in each box, like a treasure map for researchers. Some particularly special or older collections, sometimes called flagship collections, may have series and folder information too, so it's easier for researchers to find what they're searching for. Though often, on archival quests, you don't even know what you are looking for before you find it. It can be like wandering in the dark, entering as a foreign visitor on an unfamiliar shore. The best plans often disintegrate into dust like the lost papers I'd seen before.

Often these official listings and descriptions miss things. While working at Houghton in 2019, I found a sealed envelope. It was mostly free from damage, but I couldn't get it open. Adhesive, bits of water and time had sealed it firmly shut. Luckily, I was being supervised at the time by a conservation specialist. She examined my find, located supplies, and commenced her work. With meticulous precision, the conservationist lifted the envelope onto a papered surface. She unrolled a holder with a selection of tools that looked like a surgeon's scalpel collection, and used a tiny silver knife with a thin, tapered tip to carefully and patiently enter into a small gap in the adhesive. She delicately opened the envelope seal, separating adhesive from paper tiny bit by bit. I remember holding my breath as she barely blinked. It was one of the most remarkable things I'd ever seen, but in that moment, I reflected on what an archive was again. As students stomped over the grounds of the campus, did they know? There was something as special as that envelope beneath them and it wasn't just the library tunnels. It was there in the silence.

I still have much work to do with archives in the United States and at Harvard, but I always wish I could do this work with my own family history. My father is gone, my grandfather is gone, his mother is gone, my mother is gone. Everyone faded into memory. The archives I work in at Houghton are still here. Now in crisp Paige-brand acid-free and calcium-carbonate buffered archive boxes, they've been cleaned and protected. Resisting even the slightest changes in pH, they are now meticulously preserved. So much is involved in keeping things safe and unchanged in a place like this. Everyone here thinks about how paper leaks out chemicals over time and, when not properly stored, can deteriorate rapidly. But this physical knowledge of storage and preservation practice leaves us with an important message beyond the scientific specificities. If we want to preserve the past, we have to work at it. If we stop thinking about the past and working to keep it safe, it won't be there for us to come back to. While our physical archival history needs to be cared for, catalogued, preserved and stored in a way that allows it to be accessed by the generations who come after us, we must consider the rest of the story. We must search the silence for voices and stories that aren't on the page.

We must remember the living archive around us.

3

In the Company of Poets

Like Hart Crane, I remember much forgetfulness.
His birds and words in perfect flight, proving that ground
and poetry can fill the emptiness.

We wake, we eat, we shower and dress.
Each day brings a cold new blight
but poetry is solace, it soothes the emptiness.

Ginsberg's volume howls to us among those who jest,
don't fear what lurks in the supermarket night.
Poetry above all else can fill the emptiness.

Frost offers to cool and mend the best.
Wrap his words around you and he'll help you fight.
He climbed Crane's bridge and his forgetfulness.

Dickinson calls from her attic nest,
there's safety in the syllables! She shines white bright.
Poetry, if embraced, is a salve for loneliness.

When I find myself in a word-filled wilderness,
I've gotten something in my small life right.
Like Crane, I can remember much forgetfulness.
But I know the souls of the poets. They fill my emptiness.

Diana *for Diana Der Hovanessian*

Now,
you're mythology.
Then,
I sat with apology.

I'm sorry to trouble you *here*.
Your arms and home are open to me
as are your eyes.

Armenia,
Your grandfather telling you it needed journalists.
You told stories in poetry.

Lowell's last poetry class at Harvard,
You were there and you sing that song to me.

While you wobble, I see the glimmer in your eye.
The body betrays but you don't lose the rhyme.

I wonder, you say, how I wonder if you might,
down basement stairs you show me wonderland.

Dusty boxes hiding there for days and weeks and years,
I hold history in my hands.

The dust makes me sneeze, eyes water for a different reason.
My curiosity salivates, an archive is *there*.

Into your home I was invited, down those treasure stairs.
Then it would all begin, years and years of making others care.

We fought the mould and dusted pages.
Twenty-first century cleaning kept them frozen there.

And now, in the depository, they're deposited.
Diana, I made sure of it, they'll always be there.

Professor John Holmes

You taught her
Now me
The Writing of Poetry
Tufts teacher traipsing
Across Boston streets
Beantown is a breeze
Elected king of hearts in '59
A club of poetry just for you
In '65 you're at the White House
At ease at the Festival of Arts

But she bled on your papers
Though, on the lumbar of your chair
Did you watch with your cigar?
Was I not supposed to know about her?

They're peering around Somerville doors
Seven collections couldn't make it right, you know
Teaching all those classes to students writing more and more
Professor you speak to me though, I forgive, she would, I'm sure

You teach me
Be tidy with words
Don't enquire further
Close those Somerville doors
Sexton's there lurking behind those though
She's knocking with blood stains on her car floor

Melancholy Lady *for Sylvia Plath*

So, it begins, again.
Once every ten days
I manage it –

My reverse miracle, catastrophe.
Dissociative amnesiac,
My right hand

Is wordless,
My face of effacement
Delicately disappearing.

Remove my skin.
Dear one, see inside.
Do I terrify?

My memories, mistakes, a box of matches?
The moth breath
Is the only thing to stay.

So, it carries on.
Once every ten days
I manage it –

Soon, too soon
To synchronise my eyes
To falling skies

And I a smiling writer.
I am only forty.
But over and over, I have died.

The blood thump is freed.
What fun it is
To annihilate my heart.

So, it continues.
Once every ten days
I manage it –

I am the same, fractured woman.
The first time it happened, I was a teen.
It came by surprise.

The second time while
Not welcome, it called and
I was as shut

As a wound. Waiting.
So they sold my wild
And I purred while the cat was away.

Now I perform.
Once every ten days
I manage it –

Waiting to die
Artistically, is something else.
I'm very good at that.

I do it until I fall flat.
I let the buoyancy float.
I'm an emotional plutocrat.

It's simple enough to do it in a room.
It's simple enough to do it and stay neat.
It's the simplistic

Slip back into the light of mind,
Living in the same place
It was before:

I'm free,
An insensible shout.
It knocks them out.

So, I move on.
Once every ten days
I manage it –

I pay the fee, crying. A discounted rate
For the hummingbird heart –
The speed.

There's always a fee, a price for me
Going into it again,
Or a bit of flesh

or the bell of a song, or my voice.
So, so, docteur,
I'm my own enemy.

So, I turn to sleep.
Once every ten days
I manage it –

I am your Benzedrine,
I'm benzodiazepine,
The rested child

That isn't here anymore.
I move and I lose.
Don't think I overexaggerate the general abuse.

Friend, friend –
you stir me and I purr.
but under the skin flap there is nothing there.
A pair of blue eyes,

A blonde ponytail,
A platinum ring.
Ange déchu, I'm here for you.

Mapping Elizabeth

You aren't quite the same, Miss Bishop,
as the Mrs pair of Confessional tricks
not part of a triptych.
Beautiful artifice, you were the one who
mastered the art of losing.

Others lost indeed, but spoke in decibels.
Your murmurs softly knelled.
Drafts laboured on, over and over.
Scrawls like snails' glitters on a clover.

You mastered the art of losing,
Lota's Brazilian pleas.
Wooed with waterfalls over mountains,
a place for you to be free.

But you lost the freedom and your art.
Took to the shadows and kept Alice there,
soothing the throat with liquor
until even your voice wasn't fair.

In your youth, you had greyed, but Lowell
was transfixed by your reticent spell.
Your words came with magic and moments
with no replicas of passion quelled.

Mind gave in to disaster
when your blood pushed farther and faster.
Your cities, your realms and continents.
Loss, you had finally mastered.

Treasures *for Victor Howes*

In the picture
I have of you, you sit listening
head low
your ears to the air,
searching for the songs of shells
and muses.

Even in black and white I can see the polished shine
on your shoes
the well-cut suit
the woolly socks with your knees
one locked over the other.
You were
so young, so large
you stooped
the words spiral around you.

You listened to history that day
which later, I would do with you.

Across the table at an afternoon tea, you shared it with me
I remember a small moment of you.

Now no accolades remain, no Nobel or Pulitzer,
just your name on papers
your voice in mind
your body stooping from age.

There are newspaper clippings that fall to pieces in my hands,
your copies of Frost I couldn't fit in my suitcase.
How I cried knowing what they had been to you,
what they meant to me.

I stroked your bookshelf
your reading chair, seeing you sitting
there, I won't forget that spiralling staircase.
Back Bay place,
what it must have meant to you.

You remain a faded king, a lover of arts,
among the pages of the books I borrowed.
But there's no one to give them back to
now, only unarchived sorrow.

I'd have liked to have seen your eyes glow again.
Heard more about the times you'd borrowed their time
like I borrowed yours, like I'll pass on mine.

But we are both part of the symmetry
The lines the New England Poetry Club
left behind.

Lizzie and Cal

There's a line where she holds her pillow to her hollows like a child
And you do nothing to soothe her ache
The magnolias bloom and then die in their white
and you write

A Beacon Hill Back Bay kind of life
Chaise longue with books in piles
Generational burdens and dusty curtains
She cares for it all
and you write

Twenty-one years together
Sped up and manic, you tested her ten times
Fifteen times locked in the hospitals
She visits again
and you write

The shocks, water blasts, the lithium
The roads to doom and back, salvation
She salved and said amen
and you wrote

The glory called you across the pond
You left her behind
Stealing her words
so you'd write

Then one night, taxi bright
You were there again
She waited to see you
write

But with a picture of her
You left the stage
And all the while
she wrote

Arrowroot *for my mother*

The crisp tiny ovals
I thought of them today, far away

me sitting cross-legged
bench side

with your third eye

You were cooking without a care
stirring the bowl of powdered sugar

I, holding back the thumb
watched it all glisten like ripe fruit
only sweeter

We'd sugarcoat the pansies, press them into biscuit
tender voices and fingers
but your words would go unsweetened

Mumma's little girls
you'd say about those flowers
planting them

ready
every spring
the delicacy of an angel

I'd watch the freckles on the back of your hands
match the freckles on the back of my hands

I can still feel the teeth crush
biting when the icing set
gleaming shell
my mouth wet

It seemed things would always be this way

I should have made those biscuits for you
bedside

pressed the sugar sweetness to your dry mouth
in those final days

You cried out for water then
nurses scolding us for the straw
She can't swallow anymore

But how could the flowered fortress fade?
you were my great tap root

Feeding, creating, breathing
my moon and my stars
repeating

I was you
I still am
my voice echoes you in every vowel
but you were also my place to shoot off from

I followed my arrow
and you wept
I just don't understand you
and I kept
the secrets in my heart

As a child, every day
you'd ask me
by juice and milk,
radio playing
what I wanted for breakfast

The warmth from your floral dressing gown
offered treasures to be found
in your most vulnerable embrace

The brekkie bikkies, please
the arrowroot

Safety
consistency
fallacy

Empty wheat
believing they were something more

What did you think I'd be
I said as a young woman, still curious me
heart light, breast proud, expecting praise for all
Married by now, with children
and I wept

As my own woman, no children or husband beside, I replied

> *I've always wondered when people settle down what*
> *they choose to hide*

I watched your tiny chest breathe painfully,
crackling sounds,
bleeding eyes

Where was your third eye then?
wandering somewhere blind

I held your mottled hand
and cried

I knew you were proud
of me and of us and the heft of two hearts
married in a different way
the distillation of your face and voice and freckled hands
sweetened vapour now
I carry you on

The little flowers died on the day you went away
but I thought of them today

4

On the T. Part 2

A masterpiece
with a strip of sun to keep us from edging
over inlaid arches of grime
tiled paradise forgotten by time.

The bleeps and taps of Charlie transit cards.
Into the enclaves we go,
silver poles on a red line
inbound, outbound, does anyone know?

An American subway is a thing to adore
but I stumble and fear it sees me,
how I identify.
I'm not American, I'm a fake. Not
like a diner, a flag, a pecan pie,
but I try them on for size.

Clutching a pole, searching for a seat
a boy carries a pumpkin,
it's Halloween.

I avoid the cold and ride for one stop
in this city of walkers wearing L.L.Bean.

I'm a foreigner
in a masterpiece
waiting to be seen.

Kind of Like Her

for Anne Sexton and her archives

Today, I listen to tapes, therapy recordings, distant cries.
Cigarettes light on grainy black and white.

I'm being paid to enter, they pay my toll, I'm in her mind.
Familiar fortress I see her floating, a witch, headless in the night.

It's nice to meet you, I say silently, she's distant. Nothing there.
But I listen and listen and listen for hours,
Three hundred, day after day I'm there.

Twelve fingers she reaches out to me, clutches my throat, pulls
my hair.
You're like me, she says, and I blush reddishly.
She's dark on the outside, on the outside I'm fair,

But dark on the inside I hear her possession song.
Crashing into the caves, I bleed and I tear.

She breaks me down with her blackness,
All the black I've known,
and she still scares.

Today, I listen to tapes, I don't dance. There's no singing here.
Or back there.

But in her mind, as Her Kind, I find
the broken nursery rhymes
and I scare.

Sonnet Remembering You

for Edna St. Vincent Millay

Among the thistles and figs I see
Fire-haired calligraphy and pavement squares
In Greenwich finding meaning in the trees
Forlorn I mourn your death on devil stairs.
You're not all done forever; by and by
I won't forget you, I must say my vow
Your treats of sweet word flowers make me wise
Elfin angel in the blueberries now.
Biologically speaking, you're dust
No steeple on top of the life you held dear
Just dresses that hang limp in their rust
Now, it's my day, my time, my half a year.
Will we all find the words we are seeking?
It's pointless, metaphysically speaking.

Lines

In this climate never void of
incisive seasons,
I open my palm and follow the lines.
The centre point is a dime.
I have a room, a pay cheque. Check.
A gift given to me by the institutions
who have taken so much. Been locked
by the people with skin like snowflakes,
but the white snow is a gift.
Anglican hymns fill my ears like the prefix.
The Saxon conquerors of Harvard Square
pray like the Protestants who
fix their rent as high as their privilege.
But they tell me of the opportunity,
how the city, the country, is *mine*
if I Dream.
I produce and please and write
but don't rhyme,
forget the music of my own Dreamtime.
Think, they say, contribute something of worth.
Irrelevant if it isn't written down, researched.
Colour within, not outside your songs, our lines.

The Puritans push into my sleep, we wrestle, and I climb
back into the lines on my palms, the songs, which shoot off in
four directions.
One not covered with snow.
Here, the mysteries of the other peoples don't matter,
they'll tell me who's important.

The walls keep some in and some out.

The Urban Literate

Gingerbread houses are all I see.
The dormered roof
pitched, porched privacy.
Commissioned history.
I find myself amongst it
in the sitting room reading poetry.

Another page of this book
is written each day on red cobblestone.
Now, I am a part of the history
of this literary urban geography.

I scan library shelves looking for me.
For my people. My country.
But lost underneath the globe,
we sit forgotten on desks of mahogany.

I'm invited to dinner and tea
with intellectual conversation.
Be careful of fickle preoccupations,
only port after spatchcock for me.

Cambridge courts me and I'm squared.
Porter, Kendall, Central unaware.
So left they lean onto castles
that tumble into heirs.

I join the brigade. The revolution. I
find my solutions in this absolution.
But I know there is more to speak:
Boston, buyer beware.

Memory Book

History's residue in book spines.
My eyes carefully scan the view.
Library shelves with their coded keys have always meant sweet sanctuary.

I've been solo.
So lonely.
Ceaselessly trapped in any given tragedy.

Then I've pulled out a book,
read stories anew.
Rebirth. I make it through.

It's been this way as long as I remember.
Something I never outgrew.
Like some kind of haunting alchemy,
bringing gifts to me and peacefully. So,
I find it reassuring, knowing others can do this too
and will so wilfully.

But there's still something missing in those libraries.

There's no story written of you.

Formidable. Unforgettable. I swore I'd write your story one day.
A hero as worthy as the sagas of lore.
You were never outmatched in how I adored.
But my memories now just footnote what you saw, your heart, all you were.

I smell Brylcreem and diesel spills on sun-brown skin.
I sit and wait on the garage floor.
Then the roar of the truck, jump up and squeal so happily,
Daddy's home once more.

Your sanctuary was alone by the river.
You'd have to go every two months or so.
Was it a Walkabout? The water your books.
A meditation?
It was essential is all I know.

Shoulders strong from the weight of lucerne
then hours of truck driving took their toll.
You'd even been a drover, you told me once.
My awe for you daily grown.

But what about the past?

Before my brothers,
your brothers.
Some I'd come to know.

But it would be through the pain I'd learn about that history.
You'd try to keep it alone.
There was the violence.
The drink.
The poverty.
Dirt for floors.
Now, so grateful for our home.
Mum's floral curtains framed a window,
and I'd watch you tinkering,

My father with a poet's soul.

Are you why I hear only ballads?
The answer I already know.
You helped me listen, cart wood and talk to trees,
the birds with all the colours show.

There are so many pages.
I could write a book-long elegy.
I miss you is all I know.

Thank you for my heart,
for my memories.
What you sowed still grows.

Lobotomy

Suboptimal lobe. A frontal affront.
The lying leucotomy. The pick, cure.
Nobel Prize-winning drill into head, blunt.
Ethanol spills in skulls that streak to pure.

Terrorised thousands find stars to twist their wish.
Moniz says with ease, *Just watch this.*
In globed bowls like bubbling baffled fish,
Freeman and Watts look to their eyes and raise the pick.

How many thoughts in minds would have been spared?
Songs and stories and lives lived
without psychosurgical saviours. Chop, chip

chunks and clinks over bone
into shards. *Should have left them alone*, they say.
But for the answers they prayed,
now their days will be gay
and their minds firmly moored in granite.

Orbital lobotomy!

Everything you see
will be 1950s suburban glee.
Pull down the posters.
Set down the picks.
No mental castration for me.

Veritas

open ye the gates
that the righteous nation which keepeth the truth
may enter in

fumble thee with the locks
on what Katharine Lee Bates tells us is beautiful
welcome thee in

thine bombs and thine atoms
rattle the hinges around the edges
run back in

thy red and thy blue hands
covered in irony-dripping patriotism
maybe thou wilt drive in

women climb thy wall
dustbins asunder acid thrown all over the door
burning its way

thine dollar, dollar bills
overconsumption fills shelves top to floor
seeping down

closing gates
colours filtered through state lines and chasms
walling us in

watch it all tumble and fall
welcome to post-truth America free and brave
it's time to get out

Pages

In this room of studious pastimes,
the Sun isn't auditioning or cast from any window.
But woodgrain glows under pages
underground this library cave is a shrine.

I look for twentieth century ideas,
but the books that press themselves against
glass casings are fourteen hundred breaths
after death.

I smooth and shush my own pages,
rocking them and their memories and aching cries.
There are people in the storied shapes of ages.
I can see skin and teeth when I tilt my eyes.

An archive is living and the dead. I touch
this hallowed ground with my hands.
Others walk over graves with their feet,
not seeing the vestige coating my mind.

I try
to remember

their minds and their hearts and their breathing
that worms and warns me time is finite.
I'll be nothing soon enough they say (courageous)
left alone in shelved spaces.

ACKNOWLEDGEMENTS

This collection would not exist without my beloved parents, who opened my eyes to the profound beauty that lives in every corner of human experience, and my big brother Jamie, who helps me keep seeing it every day. Mum and Dad – your voices echo through these pages, and I carry your hearts with me always. Thanks to Charles and Marlene, Kylie and Gen, and all my family and friends. To my beautiful husband Stephen: in you and your love, I have found a forever home. To my baby Arielle, as you begin to write your own life, may you love words as much as we love you.

My gratitude goes to Kent MacCarter, whose faith, patience and keen editorial eye helped this collection happen. Thank you to all my academic colleagues at Australian National University and beyond. To my writing friends and mentors, thank you for believing in me and helping me along with this passion we all follow. Thank you to Deborah Durie for your unwavering grace and wisdom.

Thanks also to the New England Poetry Club, particularly Mary Buchinger, Linda Haviland Conte, Hilary Sallick and the late Diana Der Hovanessian and Victor Howes. All of your kindnesses, generosity and trust in me over the years has always made me feel welcome.

This work – and my life in Boston – would not have been possible without the generous support of numerous institutions, especially Harvard University. The Arthur and Elizabeth Schlesinger Library on the History of Women in America provided the dissertation fellowship that first brought me to Boston, while the Houghton Library also supported my research with a fellowship.

I owe particular thanks to the archives, libraries and their staff whose patient guidance has always sustained me – from the

Boston Public Library to the Forbes Public Library, Lilly Library, Massachusetts Historical Society, Smith College and their Mortimer Rare Book Room, Poet's House in New York and the Woodberry Poetry Room.

Thank you to the University of Wollongong for my education, particularly Anne Collett and Louise D'Arcens.

Finally, to Boston, the city I love. This collection would not exist without it – its streets, buildings, trees, water, art and history. This endlessly fascinating palimpsest and its enduring spirit has shaped every poem within these pages.

Sarah-Jane (SJ) Burton fell in love with reading and writing poetry as a child, discovering worlds within words that shaped how she saw everything around her.

Burton holds a BA and an MA in English and a PhD in 20th century American poetry. She is currently a Research Fellow in English at the Australian National University and has been published in academic journals and popular media both domestically and internationally. She has taught English, media studies and creative writing since 2009, and has also worked in the tertiary library sector and in university communications management and Indigenous education. Her work has been supported by grants from multiple universities including Harvard University, Indiana University, the University of Wollongong and Western Sydney University. Having lived and worked in the United States periodically over the last 15 years, notably in Boston and New England, Burton brings a cross-cultural perspective to her poetry. She draws from both her Indigenous and European heritage in her work, exploring themes of place, identity and belonging. She currently lives in regional New South Wales with her husband and little ones.